Ninety-five Theses

for the Contemporary Church

*Challenging the contemporary Church
to a reaffirmation of its historic beliefs
and a re-examination of its ecclesial
practices and exhortations*

C.I.Y. Publishing
P.O. Box 1822
Fallbrook, California 92088-1822

NINETY-FIVE THESES
FOR THE CONTEMPORARY CHURCH

© 2009 by James A. Fowler
Revised © 2010 by James A. Fowler

Published by
C.I.Y. Publishing
P.O. Box 1822
Fallbrook, California 92088-1822

ISBN 978-1-929541-54-6

Scripture quotations are from the New American Standard Bible, Copyright © 1960, 1962, 1963, 1968, 1971, 1972, 1973, 1975 by The Lockman Foundation, LaHabra, California.

Printed in the United States of America

Introduction

It Has been almost 500 years since Martin Luther
posted his ninety-five theses on the door of the castle
church in Wittenberg on October 31, 1517. Two months
prior to that posting, on September 4, 1517, Luther had
written, and sent to the Augustinian monastery in
Erfurt, ninety-seven theses against scholastic theology.
He was stonewalled – there was no reaction or response
to his statements. In October of 1517 Martin Luther
wrote his list of ninety-five theses against indulgences.
This time he collaborated with his friend Lucas Cranach
(the elder), a painter and printer living in Wittenberg.
The ninety-five theses were reportedly posted on the
door of the castle church in Wittenberg, but more
importantly they utilized the relatively new
communication medium of movable type and printing,
whereby printed copies of the ninety-five theses were
distributed to major churches and universities
throughout the region, and even as far as Rome.
Utilizing the methodological means of contemporary

technological media, the ninety-five theses made a major impact on the entire church and changed the course of Western history.

In formulating this list of ninety-five theses for the contemporary church, and utilizing the latest of technological tools for their distribution and dissemination, we could wish that these theses might have as great an impact. Our objective is to challenge the contemporary institutional church to reconsider some of its teaching and practice. These thesis statements are not intended to be just another critical complaint against the contemporary church, but they are published as a positive declaration of the Christian gospel of Jesus Christ, with accompanying correctives that might be addressed.

Some will object to this challenge of the ecclesiastical status quo, thinking that in critiquing the thought and practice of the church we are casting doubts about Christianity or even denigrating the gospel of Jesus Christ. Not so! Earlier in the year 1517, prior to his posting his original ninety-five theses on the Wittenberg Castle Church door, Martin Luther stated in one of his sermons, "Where Christ is, there He will always go against the flow." This is a most insightful and significant statement. The living Lord Jesus Christ is not content with the status-quo of "business as usual," and will always counter the routine of religion in order to assure a dynamic and spontaneous expression of His ever unique and novel work in Christian individuals and in His church.

The theses enumerated below contain both theological and methodological statements, addressing both the teaching and the practice of the Christian community. Several of the initial statements are reiterations of the historic creedal assertions of the Church, which must be maintained and reaffirmed. Several of the subsequent theological theses challenge the interpretations of some of the subsidiary tenets of Christian thought. Following the theological considerations, attention is turned to the praxis of the Christian life and various practices in the ecclesiastical communities. Many of the ministry methods employed in the contemporary church are abominably misrepresentative of the gospel of Jesus Christ and need to be challenged and reconsidered.

What response might we expect? A "new reformation" will not be an adequate response or reaction. To attempt to rebuild upon the present crumbling religious superstructure by re-forming existing policies and ideological systems is to invite disaster. The situation requires a complete restoration of the grace dynamic of the gospel of Jesus Christ, whereby the "old wineskins" (Matthew 9:17) of the religious status-quo are discarded and the "new wine" of the living Lord Jesus is allowed to fill Christian individuals and the collective expression of the Church.

These ninety-five theses for the contemporary Church are written with the sincere desire that the reality of the living Lord Jesus and the genuine manifestation of His life in His Body, the Church, might be allowed full expression by the power of God's Spirit. May the Church of Jesus Christ cease to "quench the Spirit" (I Thess. 5:19) and "grieve the Spirit" (Ephesians 4:30), as God continues to "fill with His Spirit" (Eph. 5:18) and fully reveals Himself within His new creation unto His own glory (II Peter 1:3).

Preface

Jesus explained that the gates of hell/*hades* shall not ultimately prevail against His church (Matthew 16:18) and the Christian faith. That does not mean that distortion and misrepresentation do not pervade and infect the temporal expression of the *ecclesia*. Our prefatory premise is that this present situation of the church should be addressed and corrected, and to that end we do hereby set forth this series of theses to be considered by God's people.

We respect the historic expressions of the Christian faith from previous generations. The time-honored statements of the Apostles' Creed, the Nicene Creed, and the Athanasian Creed should not be jettisoned, but retained as valid expressions of Christian orthodoxy, whereby we "contend for the faith once and for all delivered to the saints" (Jude 1:3). These present theses do not contradict or deny the scripturally documented ecclesiastical consensus of the past.

We invite all who call themselves "Christians" to consider and discuss the following theses. May such discussion be conducted in "the love (Romans 15:30) and unity (Ephesians 4:3) of the Spirit" that "we might all attain to the unity of the faith, and of the knowledge of the Son of God, to a mature man, to the measure of the stature which belongs to the fullness of Christ" (Ephesians 4:13). "Come, let us reason together" (Isaiah 1:18).

Thesis #1

Trinitarian monotheism is the distinctive and indispensable Christian concept of God. In contrast to the monadic monotheism of Judaism and Islam, the Christian faith recognizes God as essentially one Being who eternally exists in three persons – Father, Son, and Holy Spirit – a tri-unity identified as the divine Trinity. This is not to be construed as a polytheistic tri-theism, or as a monadic modalism wherein the three divine Persons are but modes of manifestation or role-function.

Thesis #2

Consideration of God must commence with His **divine character** of righteousness, goodness, mercy, love, etc. What/Who God *is*, only God *is*. The singularity of His holiness separates Him from all that is not Him. Who He *is* is not determined by what He *does*, rather, He *does* what He *does* because He *is* Who He *is*. His action is always in absolute consistency with the character of His Being, and His Being is implicit within and always expressed by His every action.

Thesis #3

The divine **Son of God**, the Word, became flesh (John 1:14) in the historic incarnation, voluntarily emptying Himself (Philippians 2:7) of any prerogative of divine function in order to function as a human bondservant in the likeness of sinful humanity (Romans 8:3). Fully God and fully man in the unity of one Person, the God-man served as "the one mediator between God and man" (I Tim. 2:5), reconciling receptive humanity to God (II Corinthians 5:19).

Thesis #4

Functioning not of divine initiative, but allowing God the Father to function in and through His humanity (John 14:10), Jesus was "obedient unto death, even **death on a cross**" (Philippians 2:8). By crucifixion Jesus "paid the price" (I Cor. 6:20; 7:23) of the death consequence of humanity's sin. As a sinless sacrifice, dying as the representative substitute for all mankind, He "could not be held in death's power" (Acts 2:24), and rose triumphant over death in the resurrection.

Thesis #5

The divine **Holy Spirit**, consubstantial
with the Father and the Son, and the expressive
spiration of both Father and Son, was "poured
out" (Acts 2:17,18) in availability to all mankind
on Pentecost. The "Spirit of God" (I Cor. 3:16),
the "Spirit of Christ" (Rom. 8:9), was thereby
available as the indwelling witness to the
human spirit (Rom. 8:16), effecting spiritual
regeneration (John 3:6) and energizing both the
"fruit" (Gal. 5:22) and the "gifts of the Spirit" (I
Cor. 12:1) in Christian lives.

Thesis #6

God alone has **"free will"** – the ability and freedom to Self-determine His own action in accord with His own character, and the subsequent inherent power to Self-implement the expression of such character in action. God created human beings as choosing creatures, granting them the freedom of choice and responsibility (response-ability) to choose or reject to be receptive to God's power and action in their lives, accepting the consequences thereof.

Thesis #7

God is absolute in character, independent in operation, and auto-generative in expression. God created human beings as dependent creatures, contingent upon a spirit-source (God or Satan) to derive all character, and to energize all active expression of behavior. The response-ability of all human beings is to make the necessary choices of receptivity (faith) that allow for active spiritual expression. This is counter to all humanistic premises of self-actualization and self-potential.

Thesis #8

The triune living God is the **creative source** of all life. Life cannot be derived from non-life. God created human beings in such a way that His divine life might dwell within humanity and provide the source of all life and character. Jesus identified Himself as "the life" (John 14:6) that He came to make available to all humanity (John 10:10) by His own indwelling presence (I John 5:12,13) as the "life-giving Spirit" (I Cor. 15:45), "the Lord, the Spirit" (II Cor. 3:17,18).

Thesis #9

The infinite and eternal God is beyond the full comprehension and understanding of the finite knowledge of mankind. He ever remains an unknowable mystery (*apophatic* theology). On the other hand, God intends that humanity might know Him, and has engaged in the Self-revelation of Himself in natural creation, by the incarnation of His Son, Jesus Christ, and in the written record of the scriptures. **God is knowable** (*kataphatic* theology), not merely intellectually, but relationally.

Thesis #10

Lucifer (Isaiah 14:12) was an angelic spirit-being, a choosing derivative creature designed to serve as a messenger to "bear God's light" unto God's glory. In selfish rebellion, desiring to be "like the Most High God" (Isaiah 14:14), he inexplicably chose to oppose God. In so doing, he became **Satan**, the devil, the adversary, the fixed antithetical negative to God's positive character, perverting that which is of God and "making crooked the straight ways of God" (Acts 13:10)

Thesis #11

When **God created** human beings as the
highest order of His creation, He "breathed into
them the breath (spirit) of His life" (Gen. 3:7),
allowing humanity, male and female (Gen. 1:27)
to live in "spirit, and soul, and body" (I Thess.
5:23) by deriving life and character from the
divine presence within their spirit. Human
beings are not independent and self-generative,
but are always contingent creatures deriving
spiritual condition, nature, identity and
character from a spiritual source.

Thesis #12

Human beings were designed by the Creator God to function spiritually, psychologically, and physiologically. "May the God of peace sanctify you entirely, and may your **spirit** and **soul** and **body** be preserved complete, without blame at the coming of the Lord Jesus Christ" (I Thess. 5:23). Human beings are not dissected or subdivided into three parts, partitions or compartments (trichotomous or tripartite), but are designed to function as God intended at three levels of life.

Thesis #13

Humanity was created "in the **image of God**" (Genesis 1:26,27). This should not be construed to mean that there is something about mankind that is intrinsically like God. The "image of God" is not a static attribution of divine characteristics to the creature, but a derived image whereby the invisible character of God can be made visible in human behavior when the individual becomes a "new man" in Christ, thus allowing correspondence with the "image of the Creator" (Colossians 3:10).

Thesis #14

Representing the human race, the original couple, **Adam and Eve,** were deceived by the Deceiver into making a choice against deriving all from their Creator. They did not become independent, self-generative beings, "like God" (Gen. 3:5), as the diabolic Liar suggested, but instead were thereafter dependent upon Satan for their spiritual identity as "sinners" (Romans 5:21), and for the selfish and evil character of sin derived from the Evil One expressed as sins in their behavior.

Thesis #15

After their fall into **sin**, manifesting character contrary to the character of God derived from the devil (I John 3:8), humanity was not essentially, inherently or intrinsically sinful. Human beings did not become devils. In their fallen, depraved spiritual condition, separated from God (Isa. 59:2) and "devoid of the Spirit" (Jude 1:19), the whole world of fallen humanity lies in the Evil One (I John 5:18), who is "the spirit who works in the sons of disobedience" (Eph. 2:2).

Thesis #16

God's statement to the first couple, "you will surely die" (Gen. 2:17), was not necessarily a threat of a vindictive penalty for disobedient, misbehavioral sin. The inevitable alternative of deriving from God's life was to derive from "the one having the power of death, that is the devil" (Heb. 2:14). "Alienated from the life of God" (Eph. 4:18), **spiritual death** came upon all mankind because of Adam's sin (cf. Rom. 5:12-21), and as a consequence all were "dead in trespasses and sins" (Eph. 2:1,5).

Thesis #17

The redemptive death of Jesus Christ has been explained by numerous atonement theories. Jesus "gave His life a ransom for many" (Matt. 20:28), and by His death "bought with a price" (I Cor. 6:23; 7:20) our "eternal **redemption**" (Heb. 9:12). Economic redemption without relational restoration is an empty transaction. Jesus' voluntary death as our kinsman-redeemer (cf. Ruth 2:20; 4:14) emancipated humanity to participate in the relational restoration of a full inheritance with God.

Thesis #18

Christian teaching has long emphasized the **cross of Christ** (I Cor. 1:17). The Roman execution instrument on which Jesus died became a symbol of "Christ crucified" (I Cor. 1:23; 2:2) and His "finished work" (Jn. 19:30) on behalf of all humanity. Christians are identified in Christ's crucifixion (cf. Rom. 6:6; Gal. 2:20), but must beware of making the cross-symbol into a fetish with alleged intrinsic power, or of investing the cross-symbol with the power to save or mortify.

Thesis #19

The phrase "**blood of Christ**" refers to the "death of Christ," effective for redemption (Eph. 1:7), propitiation (Rom. 3:25), justification (Rom. 5:9), reconciliation (Col. 1:20), and access to God (Eph. 2:13) – the basis of the new covenant (Heb. 13:20). Christians must be cautious of elevating the idea of Jesus' blood into a sacred substance with intrinsic divine power contacted in sacramental involvement or employed by the mantra of "pleading the blood."

Thesis #20

The need of fallen humanity was not
rehabilitation, regulatory restructuring, or
religion. Each human individual needs to be re-
lifed with the divine life of the triune God.
Spiritual death must be replaced with the
spiritual life of Jesus Christ (I John 5:12). Jesus
explained, "You must be born from above" (John
3:3,7). Spiritual **regeneration** is the
restoration, the "bringing into being again," of
God's life in man, as we are "born again to a
living hope by the resurrection of Jesus Christ"
(I Pet. 1:3).

Thesis #21

To be identified as a "Christian" is to have received "**Christ in you**" (Col. 1:26). "If any person does not have the Spirit of Christ, he is none of His" (Rom. 8:9). Paul explains, "It is no longer I who live, but Christ lives in me" (Gal. 2:20), and "for me to live is Christ" (Philippians 1:21). Every Christian should have a clear awareness that "Christ is their life" (Col. 3:4), for Paul asks the Corinthians, "Do you not recognize that Jesus Christ is in you, unless you believed in vain?" (II Cor. 13:5).

Thesis #22

Regeneration of spirit effects a spiritual union with the Lord Jesus Christ. "He who is joined to the Lord becomes one spirit with Him" (I Cor. 6:17). The biblical analogies of husband and wife (Eph. 5:22-33) and the vine and the branches (John 15:1-6) illustrate this union. This mystic **union with Christ**, both individual and collective, must not be construed as an essential or mathematical oneness, but as a relational oneness of intimate communion with Christ.

Thesis #23

Justification has been improperly limited to an exclusive legal term signifying a forensic and juridical pardon, whereby God in heaven imputes or reckons Christ's righteousness to a believer, and declares or pronounces that person, "righteous." Righteousness is the character of God (Psalm 119:137), conveyed by God's grace in "the Righteous One" (Acts 3:14; 7:52), Jesus Christ, whose presence within makes the believer "righteous" (Romans 5:19; II Cor. 5:21).

Thesis #24

The work of God in Christ must not be so over-objectified as to diminish or deny the subjective work of God in the hearts of receptive persons. The Christ of history is the **Christ of experience**. There has been a tendency in some theological teaching to externally objectify the benefits of Jesus' redemptive work in legal and economic categories that has effectively denied to Christian people the restoration of the subjective indwelling presence of God, lost when mankind fell into sin.

Thesis #25

Christian **salvation** must always be in the context of the dynamic function of the living Savior, Jesus Christ. It must not be limited to the historical redemptive event of Christ's crucifixion, or to the individual experiential occurrence of regeneration. Salvation (*soteria*) is the process whereby we are "made safe" (*sozo*) from dysfunctional human expression and restored to God-intended functionality by the dynamic ontological expression of the Person and work of the Savior (*soterios*).

Thesis #26

Man-made theories of an ***ordo salutis***, the "order of events in salvation experience," are to be rejected as extra-biblical and arbitrary. Every facet of an individual's salvation experience is centered in the dynamic function of the Savior, Jesus Christ, in that particular person's life. Justification, salvation, sanctification, glorification, etc., though distinguishable in definition, are all joined in the comprehensive function of "the saving life of Christ" (cf. Rom. 5:10).

Thesis #27

Sanctification is part of the on-going process of justification and salvation. Whereas religion usually considers sanctification to be an external conformity of thought and behavior, it is better understood as the process whereby the Christian is receptive to the holy and righteous character of God in one's attitude and behavior, and is thereby "set apart" from all that is not derived from God. Thus we "share His holiness" (Heb. 12:10), and are "holy, as He is holy" (I Pet. 1:16).

Thesis #28

References to "eternal security" and "once saved, always saved" are often misleading and misunderstood. The permanence and **security of the Christian** believer "in Christ" is not based on any initiating action or response of the believer, but on the loving faithfulness of the Lord Jesus Christ to preserve those who are spiritually united with Him. "He who began a good work in you will bring it to completion at the day of Jesus Christ" (Philippians 1:6).

Thesis #29

Jesus commissioned His church to "make disciples, baptizing them in the name of the Father, the Son, and the Holy Spirit" (Matt. 28:19). **Baptism** in water is the external signification of the internal reality of having been "baptized into Christ" (Galatians 3:27) and His death (Romans 6:3). To be overwhelmed by water is intended to signify the overwhelming of the spirit of an individual by the Spirit of Christ, effecting their inclusion in the one Body of Christ (I Cor. 12:13), the Church.

Thesis #30

At the last Passover meal with His disciples (Matt. 26:26-29), Jesus inaugurated the memorial meal that Christians refer to as the "**Lord's Supper**" (I Cor. 11:20) or the "Eucharist" (meaning "thanksgiving" for God's "good grace"). Taking the bread and the cup, Jesus said, "Do this in remembrance of Me" (I Cor. 11:24,25). This remembrance is not an occasion for Christians to recall their sins, but to examine (I Cor. 11:28) the focus of their reverent remembrance of Jesus.

Thesis #31

The Lord's Supper observance has often been regarded as a sacramental rite that serves as a "**means of grace**" whereby the participant can experience the "real presence" of the living Christ. Jesus Christ Himself serves as the singular "means of grace" (cf. John 1:17) in the new covenant (Heb. 12:24), whereby God provides all humanity's needs (II Peter 1:4) by His redemptive and restorative grace that the "real presence" of the living Christ might dwell and function within the human spirit.

Thesis #32

The Christian faith was never intended to be an institutionalized **religion** with a hierarchy of human authority imposing mandates of belief and behavior. "I came that you might have life, and have it more abundantly," said Jesus (John 10:10). Christianity is not religion, but is, rather, the life of the risen Lord Jesus dwelling in Christians by His Spirit in order that His life and character might be lived out through faithful believers.

Thesis #33

The **Church** is not an institutional organization, nor is it the building used for religious meetings. The Church (*ecclesia*) is the collective gathering of Christian people in whom the Spirit of Christ lives, "called out" to "encourage one another" (Hebrews 10:25) as they participate together in the organic "Body of Christ" (Ephesians 4:12). Collectively the saints (Colossians 1:4) of the universal Church are to express the life and character of the living Lord Jesus.

Thesis #34

Church membership is a concept foreign to the Christian scriptures. The Church, the "Body of Christ" (Romans 12:5), is an organic entity expressive of the collective life of Jesus Christ, rather than an organizational structure with required membership attachment. Every Christian (i.e. every person in whom Christ dwells) is a functional member (I Corinthians 12:12-27) of the Body, integrally united with one another (Romans 12:4,5) to form the collective expression of Jesus Christ.

Thesis #35

The **kingdom** of God should not be perceived as a particular ecclesiastical group, or a physical geographical location or realm, either now or in the future. Jesus said, "My kingdom is not of this world" (John 8:36), for "the kingdom of God is within you" (Luke 17:21). The kingdom (*basileia*) of God is the dynamic reign (*basileuo*) of the Lord and King (*basileus*) Jesus Christ in the hearts of Christian persons – forever inseparable from His Being and function (*autobasileia*).

Thesis #36

The **unity** of the "one body" (Eph. 4:4) is to be "preserved" and "maintained" (Eph. 4:3). This is not necessarily to be manufactured or orchestrated by ecumenical movements seeking singularity of organizational institution. Such "unity of the Spirit" is not uniformity of opinion or practice, for there can and should be diversity in unity. Christians are to be "one," as God the Father and Son are One (Jn. 17:21), "perfected in unity" (Jn. 17:23) by the "perfect bond" (Col. 3:14) of divine love.

Thesis #37

Recognizing their common-unity in Christ, Christians participate in the **community** of faith, the Church. An independent, stand alone, "lone-ranger" Christian is an anomaly to Christian understanding. We are "in Him" together. We need one another. Christ in one desires fellowship with Christ in another. The Church is an interpersonal community wherein we "encourage one another" (Heb. 10:25) and "submit and defer to one another" (Eph. 5:21) in love.

Thesis #38

The **scriptures** are inspired by God (II Timothy 3:16), and providentially preserved as the objective written record of the life, death and resurrection of the historical Jesus and the original and apostolic record of Christian thought. They are useful for Christian instruction, and are not to be disregarded, denigrated or deprecated by Christian persons. But they are not to be deified or worshipped, and not to be equated with the living Lord Jesus in terms of authority.

Thesis #39

Many Christians refer to the scriptures as the "**word of God**," but the primary usage of that phrase in new covenant literature has reference to Jesus Christ. "In the beginning was the Word, and the Word was with God, and the Word was God" (John 1:1). "The Word was made flesh and dwelt among us" (John 1:14). Only in a secondary sense should the scriptures be referred to as the "word of God," and never in such a way as to be equated with or substituted for the living Lord Jesus.

Thesis #40

The source of **authority** in the lives of
Christian persons is not found in the
hierarchical authority of ecclesiastical
leadership, nor in the oft-posited authority of
the inspired scriptures. Jesus stated, "All
authority has been given to Me in heaven and
on earth" (Matthew 28:18). The personal
authority of Jesus' lordship over Christian lives,
contextualized by the interactive collective of
the Church, should be the primary basis of
Christians' respect and submission.

Thesis #41

Divine **predestination** is not a
mechanical or logical determinism that fails to
take into account the relational factor of human
freedom and responsibility. What "God
predestined before the ages" (I Cor. 2:17) was
centered in the mystery of His purpose (Eph.
1:11) of human participation in Christ Jesus. In
and by the Son, God "predestined us to adoption
as sons" (Eph. 1:5) and "predestined us to be
conformed to the image of His Son" (Rom. 8:29).

Thesis #42

God's **covenantal arrangements** and agreements with created humanity are "put through" (*diatheke*) by Himself, the superior party, for the good of the other parties. The covenant with Abraham (Genesis 12-15) had both a temporary physical fulfillment, as well as an ultimate eternal fulfillment in the realities effected by the Person and work of Jesus Christ. The new covenant in Christ is God's final arrangement whereby mankind is restored as "the Spirit gives life" (II Cor. 3:6).

Thesis #43

God's **promises** are all directed toward fulfillment in the Person and work of the Son of God, the Lord and Savior, Jesus Christ. "All the promises of God find their 'Yes' and 'Amen' in Him" (II Cor. 1:20), for He is the "confirmation of the promises given to the old covenant fathers" (Rom. 15:8). To seek any other fulfillment of God's promises is to deny the "finished work" (cf. John 19:30) of Jesus Christ, and to subvert the singular intent of God in His Son.

Thesis #44

Israel is a designation of the people in whom God rules (*yisra-el*). The dynamic rule of God has been given to the Son to serve as Lord over those people who are receptive in faith to Him. To identify "Israel" as an ethnic group, a political nation, or a geographical location with divinely chosen status is to pervert God's intent. "The hope of Israel" (Acts 28:20) is Jesus Christ, and only those people in whom He rules as Lord can legitimately be called "Israel" (cf. Rom. 9:6; Gal. 6:16).

Thesis #45

The **Law of God** is not a legal codification of behavioral standards, but the revelation of His character, and thereby what is contrary to His character (sin). Human attempts to keep the Law cannot produce righteousness (Gal. 2:21) or life (Gal. 3:21). The Mosaic Law has been abrogated (Heb. 8:13). The risen Lord Jesus is the living *Torah* "written on our hearts" (Heb. 8:10), fulfilling all God's Law in freedom (James 1:25) and love (Gal. 5:14) by the Spirit (Rom. 8:2).

Thesis #46

The Christian is dead to any performance requirements of Law (Gal. 2:19), and alive to the **grace of God** in Jesus Christ (Eph. 4:7) as He provides the divine dynamic to accomplish all He intends in the Christian life. Grace is much more than static "divine favor" that initiates personal salvation and serves as the threshold factor of the Christian life. Grace is the dynamic action of God in accordance with His divine character, enacted through the Son and by the Spirit.

Thesis #47

Humanity's response-ability to the grace-activity of God is **faith**. Faith is not simply believing the correct propositional truths, or even trusting in the faithfulness of God. Faith is ultimately the choice of a human individual to allow for the receptivity of God's grace-activity. "For by grace we have been saved through faith..." (Eph. 2:8). Initially faith is the receiving of the redemptive work of Christ on our behalf, and faith continues as receptivity to the activity of Christ's life.

Thesis #48

The Christian faith is **not a belief-system**, the tenets of which are to be affirmed in mental assent or consent. Nor is Christianity just one ideological option among many on which an individual might choose to take their epistemological stand. Jesus Christ is the singular mediator between God and man (I Tim. 2:5), providing access to God (John 14:6), salvation (Acts 4:12), and eternal life (John 3:15; Rom. 6:23; I John 5:11) to receptive mankind.

Thesis #49

Christianity is not an amalgam of many teachings, one of which is the study of the Person of Jesus Christ. The singular reality Jesus came to bring in His physical advent on planet earth was Himself. "I came that you might have life, and have it more abundantly" (Jn. 10:10). I AM that life (John 11:25; 14:6; I John 5:12). The Christian faith is not believing in Jesus + other accompanying tenets. Christianity IS Christ. Jesus Christ + nothing! *Sola Christos* – Christ alone!

Thesis #50

Eschatology is the study of "**last things**." It is not speculative projection of the sequence and timing of future events. God's "last thing" is His Son, Jesus Christ, "the last Adam" (I Cor. 15:45). "In these last days God has spoken to us in His Son" (Heb. 1:2). "In the last days God will pour out His Spirit on all mankind" (Acts 2:17). New covenant thought focuses on the present fulfillment of "last things" in Christ (already), while anticipating the consummation of the "last days" (not yet).

Thesis #51

The inherent **immortality** of the human soul is not part of Christian teaching. God "alone possesses immortality" (I Timothy 6:16), and "through Christ Jesus has brought life and immortality to light through the gospel" (II Timothy 1:10). Immortality in created human beings is derived from God's presence. "Those who seek immortality, He will give eternal life" (Romans 2:7), and in the bodily resurrection "the mortal shall have put on immortality" (I Cor. 15:53,54).

Thesis #52

Eternal life is not a commodity or a benefit granted to Christians after they die. Eternal life is the life of the eternally living Lord Jesus Christ received by faith. "God has given us eternal life, and this life is in His Son" (I John 5:11); "he who has the Son has life" (I John 5:12); "you may know that you have eternal life" (I John 5:13). "The free gift of God is eternal life in Christ Jesus our Lord" (Rom. 6:23), and "he who believes in the Son has eternal life" (John 3:36).

Thesis #53

The **destiny** of mankind is determined by the continuity and perpetuity of one's spiritual identification and union with either God or Satan, in heaven or hell. Christians have "tasted of the heavenly gift" (Heb. 6:4), are "blessed with all spiritual blessings in heavenly places" (Eph. 1:3), and are "partakers of a heavenly calling" (Heb. 3:1). "An everlasting fire is prepared for the devil and his emissaries" (Matt. 25:41). This dichotomy of destiny is a denial of universalism.

Thesis #54

Christians appreciate and anticipate God's **judgment**, for it does not involve punitive consequences to be feared, but the determinations of a just God to evaluate all things in His Son, Jesus Christ. "This is the judgment, that the Light has come into the world" (John 3:19). "We will all stand before God's judgment seat" (Rom. 14:10) when we "all die and face judgment" (Heb. 9:27). Jesus, "the judge of the living and the dead" (Acts 10:42) will determine the source of our works (I Cor. 3:12-15).

Thesis #55

The new covenant is the advent of a "better **hope**" (Heb. 7:19), far beyond the wishful, anticipatory yearning for that which is not yet, allowing Christians to confidently expect that the living Lord Jesus is fulfilling everything God desires. "Christ Jesus is our hope" (I Tim. 1:1). We have "Christ in us, the hope of glory" (Col. 1:27). Such "hope does not disappoint..."(Rom. 5:5), as we "fix our hope on His grace" (I Pet. 1:13) and "abound in hope by the Holy Spirit" (Rom. 15:13).

Thesis #56

The admonition to be "**filled with the Spirit**" (Eph. 5:18) has to do with wise steps (15), time spent (16) and mind-set (17). It results in the practicum of a song in one's heart (19), a thankful attitude (20), and deference toward others (21). When the Holy Spirit, the Spirit of Christ, controls Christian thought, affection, decision, and behavior the character of Christ will be evidenced. Such supernatural Spirit-control does not necessarily issue forth in perfectionism or ecstatic expressions.

Thesis #57

"The **fruit of the Spirit** is love, joy, peace, patience, kindness, goodness, faithfulness, gentleness, and the godly control of one's self" (Gal. 5:22,23). Such character expression cannot be produced by any efforts of the Christian. The "fruit of the Spirit" is the character of Christ, generated and expressed by the indwelling divine Holy Spirit. The "fruit of righteousness comes through Jesus Christ" (Phil. 1:11), and "the branch cannot bear fruit unless it abides in the Vine" (John 15:4).

Thesis #58

Many seek a sense of personal identity based in their possessions, abilities, or associations, but the deepest sense of **identity** is to be found in one's spiritual affiliation and union with a spirit-source, either God or Satan. The unregenerate, "in Adam," are identified as "sinners" (Rom. 5:19). The regenerated, "in Christ," are called "saints" (Eph. 1:18). Christians are more than just "sinners saved by grace" – they are "new creatures" (II Cor. 5:17), "citizens of heaven" (Phil. 3:20).

Thesis #59

The man of old, the "**old man**" we were in our fallen, unregenerate state, "has been crucified with Christ" (Rom. 6:6). That "old man" spiritual condition/identity has been forever "laid aside" (Eph. 4:22; Col. 3:9), and has been exchanged for a new spiritual condition/identity of a "**new man**" that the Christian has "put on" in Christ (Eph. 4:24; Col. 3:10). As "new creatures" (II Cor. 5:17), we recognize we "have been crucified with Christ; it is no longer I who lives, but Christ lives in me" (Gal. 2:20).

Thesis #60

The Christian does not have two opposing natures, despite the popular evangelical explanation that the Christian has both an "old nature" and a "new nature" in conflict with one another. To possess two natures simultaneously would create a schizophrenic being, paralyzed with paranoid uncertainty and legitimately excusing his sin as inevitable. "You were by nature children of wrath" (Eph. 2:3). "You have become **partakers of the divine nature**" (II Peter 1:3).

Thesis #61

Christians have been **made perfect** (Heb. 12:23) by the presence of the Perfect One, Jesus Christ, dwelling within and giving them a new identity (cf. I Cor. 2:6). Such a derived spiritual perfection does not imply a perfectionism that denies Christians can still choose to misrepresent who they are in Christ in sinful behavior. Behaviorally, we are "not perfect" (Phil. 3:12), and are called upon to "be perfect" (Matt. 5:48) and to be "made perfect in every good work" (Heb 13:21).

Thesis #62

The Christian becomes a "new creature wherein old things have passed away, and all things have become new" (II Cor. 5:17). All the old conditions of one's spirit have been jettisoned, and our spiritual condition is completely new "in Christ." This does not deny, however, the need for a continuous "**renewing of the mind**" (Rom. 12:2; Eph. 4:23) whereby the Spirit of Christ overcomes habituated thought and emotional patterns not consistent with the character of Christ.

Thesis #63

All Christians have residual patterns of selfishness and sinfulness in the desires of their soul. These patterned desires often become the basis of compulsive, obsessive, and addictive behaviors. The apostle Paul refers to these as "fleshly desires" (I Pet. 2:11) or "desires of the flesh" (Eph. 2:3). These references to "**flesh**" do not necessarily refer to the physical body, and it is important that Christians do not fall into the Platonic dualism that regarded the physical body as evil.

Thesis #64

Incorporating modern psychological terminology, some teaching in the church has advocated various actions to deal with the "**self**" – "denying self," "dying to self," etc. "Self" is often identified as the "old man," the "old nature," or the "flesh" within the person. Jesus did say, "If anyone wishes to come after Me, he must deny himself, and take up his cross daily and follow Me" (Luke 9:23). The self-effort of self-reform will accomplish nothing, but we must disallow selfish character.

Thesis #65

The **confession of sin** has taken many forms in Christian religion. "If we confess our sins, He is faithful and just to forgive us our sins" (I Jn. 1:9). To confess, *homologeo,* means "to say the same thing, to concur, or agree" with God that sin is contrary to His character. God's forgiveness is not contingent on human confession, for the death of Jesus Christ was singularly sufficient for the forgiveness of all sins, but acknowledgement (I Jn. 1:8) allows for experiential assurance of forgiveness.

Thesis #66

There is a constant need in the life of the Christian individual for personal **repentance**. Such repentance (*metanoia*) involves a "change of mind that leads to a change of action." This "change of mind" recognizes our inability to enact or perform the consistent outliving of the Christ-life, and recognizes that the "change of action" must entail the faithful receptivity of the activity of the life and character of the living Lord Jesus living out His life in and through us by God's grace.

Thesis #67

Many Christians engage in various procedures seeking to discover the "**will of God**" for their lives. The "will of God" is not a hidden object we try to find, a target we try to hit, nor is it a maze to be mastered. God's will is always Jesus – that the life and character of the risen Christ be lived out in Christian behavior – "living by the Spirit" (I Pet. 4:6), "from the heart" (Eph. 6:6), a life of "sanctification" (I Thess. 4:3), and "proving...what is good and acceptable and perfect" (Rom. 12:2).

Thesis #68

The Church of Jesus Christ need not fear the discoveries or theories of the scientific community, nor should it set the Christian faith in an adversarial position with **science**. As we seek to know (*scientia*) and understand the world God has created – its cosmological commencement; its laws of physics; how it has turned out (evolved) as it has; etc. – we must not retreat into a metaphysical enclave, but proclaim the teleological purpose of the created order unto the glory of God.

Thesis #69

Jesus is the "Chief Shepherd" (I Pet. 5:4; cf. Jn. 10:14; Heb. 13:10) or Pastor of the Church, in whom "all authority" (Matt. 28:18) is invested. The under-shepherds who pastor local churches must avoid claiming "**pastoral authority**" and engaging in authoritarian intimidation and shaming that constitutes pastoral abuse. There should be no elevated position and adoration as "the Lord's anointed," or setting themselves apart from laity as elite and professional clergy.

Thesis #70

Every Christian is a minister. Some are "gifted as pastors and teachers, for the equipping of the saints for the work of ministry, to the building up of the Body of Christ" (Eph. 4:11,12). This concept of servant-leadership wherein Christians are prepared for the "**ministry of all believers**" in order to overflow into the lives of others is the biblical model. The clergy/laity distinction has been a great detriment to the Church, decimating its witness and effectiveness.

Thesis #71

What many have referred to as "spiritual gifts" are but the **grace-expressions** (*charismata*) of the ministry of the living Lord Jesus in the lives of Christian people. They are not trophies of spiritual attainment, nor are they specific job-descriptions for narrowly defined function in the Body of Christ. As Jesus lives as Lord in the lives of His people, He will express Himself in ministry to others by the dynamic of divine grace in the church context where that individual has been placed.

Thesis #72

"God so loved the world that He *gave* His only Son" (John 3:16). A Christian who responds by "giving himself to the Lord" (II Cor. 8:5) then experiences the privilege of **Christian giving** as the presence of the Divine Giver dwells within and the Christian becomes the conduit of God's givingness. Such giving should not be "under compulsion" (II Cor. 9:7) of mandated legalistic tithing requirements, psychological manipulation, or attempts to repay God for what He has done.

Thesis #73

Much of the church has accepted and succumbed to the world's **standards of success**. Evaluating church growth by the false success factors of statistical analysis, by quantity rather than quality, by the number of nickels and noses, or by which group has more of "the three big Bs – buildings, budgets, and baptisms," desecrates the true nature of the Church as the Body of Christ, and destroys the objective of our "growing up in all aspects into Him who is the head, even Christ" (Eph. 4:15).

Thesis #74

Corporate **greed** has become
characteristic of the institutional church. The
fundraising gimmicks of tithing percentages,
selling indulgences, encouraging "seed-
planting," etc. are abominable. Like the
Pharisees, they are "lovers of money" (Lk.
16:14), which is "the root of all evil" (I Tim.
6:10), and antithetical to the love of God (cf.
Matt. 6:24). Jesus drove the moneychangers
from the temple (Jn. 2:14,15). Church leaders,
like Judas, have often misused monies in fiscal
irresponsibility.

Thesis #75

The Church has been charged with having an "edifice complex." For centuries the Church has sought to build ever larger, more elaborate, and more extravagant edifices. These **church buildings** are often a wasteful expenditure of the resources contributed by God's people, and are often underutilized facilities. Should we not focus on the people of God as "God's Building" (I Cor. 3:9), and put our energies and monies into "building up the Body of Christ" (Eph. 4:12)?

Thesis #76

The opposite of love is **selfishness**. This is the cancer that eats away at the loving community of God's people. There is a great need among Christians to allow the Holy Spirit to direct them in critical self-evaluation to ascertain the extent of self-orientation and self-effort in their lives. Few want to allow the divine microscope to expose their fleshly patterns and tendencies of selfish sinfulness, in order to submit these areas of their lives to the Lordship of the Spirit of Christ.

Thesis #77

It is a sad indictment on the church that
women have often been regarded and treated
as "second-class citizens" in the kingdom. The
apostle Paul clearly states, "male and female, all
are one in Christ Jesus" (Gal. 3:28). Men and
women are co-equal image-bearers (Gen. 1:27),
and when that divine imaging is restored in
regeneration men and women are co-equal
participants in the *ecclesia*. In the midst of their
equality, men and women can still celebrate the
differences in their genders.

Thesis #78

The observation has been made that when Christians typically gather for public worship on Sunday mornings, this is the most segregated segment of time during each week in our society. The issue of **race** and skin-color has been more adequately addressed in our society than in our churches. "Jew and Gentile (all races) are one in Christ Jesus" (Gal. 3:28). Peoples of all races and ethnicity should be thoroughly integrated as brothers and sisters in Christ wherever they assemble.

Thesis #79

Religion and **culture** are inevitably intertwined, and often inextricably merged. The gospel of Jesus Christ, however, is not to be identified with or connected to any cultural factors or forms. It is not to be identified with Western civilization or the customs and mores of a particular national or geographical region. The objective of the Christian gospel is not to change cultures or civilizations, but to convert individuals spiritually so as to transform them (and thereby their cultures).

Thesis #80

Many have thought that the objective of Christianity is to **save the world**. The world cannot be saved! The fallen world-system is controlled by "the ruler of this world" (John 16:11); "the god of this age, who blinds the minds of unbelievers" (II Cor. 4:4). This will be the context and the conflict of the Church until the ultimate triumph of Christ (I Cor. 15:25). Christians are "in the world, but not of the world" (Jn. 17:11,14), and share their faith in Christ with other individuals therein.

Thesis #81

Christian spirituality is not to be gauged by **emotional excitement**. Christian worship is not evaluated by the ecstasy of sensate experiences. God's working is not necessarily adjudged by visible supernatural miracles. There is nothing more supernatural that the character of Christ exhibited in the "fruit of the Spirit, which is love, joy, peace, patience, kindness, goodness, faithfulness, gentleness, and the godly control of one's self" (Gal. 5:22,23). Such cannot be counterfeited!

Thesis #82

The work of the living Lord Jesus Christ in individuals and churches cannot be formularized or programmed. Christians should avoid attempting to imitate or re-enact the methods or biographical expressions of others' success or spirituality. Everything Christ does is **unique and novel** to the particular person, group and time where He is working. His character will always be unchangeable, but His ways are innumerable and "past finding out" (Romans 11:33).

Thesis #83

Sharing one's Christian faith should be a spontaneous overflow of the life of Jesus Christ within the Christian individual. Formulaic **evangelistic procedures** designed to be confrontational and manipulative are counterproductive to Christian witness. People are primarily drawn to a loving lifestyle that exhibits the character of the living Christ. In the words attributed to St. Francis of Assisi, "Share Christ wherever you go, and if necessary – use words."

Thesis #84

The twenty-first century world is
permeated with the philosophy of **humanism**,
advocating that human beings are capable of
being the cause of their own effects by means of
their own self-potential. Christian religion has
often adopted the same fallacy of human
"works," by utilizing mottos of self-effort such
as, "God helps those who help themselves" or
"Do your best, and God will do the rest." The
Christian gospel pertains to what God does,
rather than what man does!

Thesis #85

The gospel of grace in Jesus Christ stands opposed to all performance of "**works**" to please God. If righteousness before God comes by means of performance of religious rules, then Christ died for no purpose (Galatians 2:21). The self-made religion of legalistic prohibitions has no value in checking the indulgences of the flesh (Colossians 2:23). Legalistic requirements with guilt-producing strictures of performance must be replaced with God's grace activity received by faith.

Thesis #86

Christian **obedience** is not rule-keeping performance or conformity to the behavioral expectations of any other persons. In the new covenant of God's grace in Jesus Christ, Christian obedience is not a legal, law-based performance issue, but a relational privilege of "listening under" (*hupakouo*) the directives of the Lord Jesus Christ in order to ascertain what and how He desires to live and operate through the Christian who is receptive to His activity in faith.

Thesis #87

The Christian life is not what the Christian does for God, but **what God does** in and through the Christian. Jesus said, "Apart from Me, you can do nothing" (John 15:5). "Not that we are adequate to consider anything as coming from ourselves, but our adequacy is of God" (II Cor. 3:5). To recognize that the divine grace of God in Jesus is the total provision of the Christian life does not lead to passive acquiescence, for God actively expresses His own Being in His every action.

Thesis #88

Incessant calls for increased **commitment**, dedication, consecration, and devotion are proclaimed in the pulpits of the churches. Such guilt-producing demands from God's people perpetuate the performance orientation of a "works" theology. The scriptures refer repeatedly to "committing sin," but personal "commitment" is not called for in the Bible. Instead, we are to "submit to God" (James 4:7), for whatever He is committed to be and do in us.

Thesis #89

The **Christian life is impossible**! No
human individual is qualified or capable to live
the Christian life. In that "whatever is not from
faith is sin" (Romans 14:23) and "without faith
it is impossible to please Him" (Heb. 11:6), it
might be considered sinful to keep trying to live
the Christian life by one's own effort. Only
Christ can live the Christian life! The Christian
life is always and only empowered by the grace
of God to bring into action the outliving of the
life and character of Jesus.

Thesis #90

The Christian life is not an imitation of Jesus, but is rather the **manifestation** of His life. The life of Jesus was much more than a perfect exemplary patterning to be reproduced by a process of "monkey see, monkey do" imitation. Paul explains Christian behavior as "the life of Jesus manifested in our mortal bodies" (II Cor. 4:10,11). The call to "imitate" the faithful receptivity of Jesus' life in apostolic leaders (Heb. 13:7) is for the purpose of re-presenting the life of Jesus in Christian lives.

Thesis #91

Prayer is something that Christians often talk about, but seldom engage in! Prayer is not an attempt to give God information (cf. Matt. 6:8), nor an attempt to coerce or cajole God to act in accord with our wishes (cf. Rom. 11:34). Prayer is the Christian privilege of reorienting oneself to God; listening in obedience to discern and ascertain how to be receptive in faith to what He desires to do next in our life. Perhaps the ultimate prayer is the confession to God, "I can't; only You can!"

Thesis #92

Worship patterns in much of the church have been so perverted as to be idolatrous. Focused on themselves, worshippers are concerned about what they *do* (come, sing, pray, give), how they *feel* (good, excited, entertained), or what they *get* (strength, peace, blessing). Christian worship is not limited by specified times (Sunday), procedural forms (rituals, sacraments), or geographic location (church buildings), but expresses the worth-ship of Christ's character in every action of life.

Thesis #93

Many Christians are seeking God's **blessings** in their lives, as evidenced in their supplicatory prayers and their search for priestly blessings. They fail to realize that God has already blessed them; that Christians have received everything God has to give in His Son, Jesus Christ. "God has blessed us with every spiritual blessing in heavenly places in Christ Jesus" (Eph. 1:3). "His divine power has granted us everything pertaining to life and godliness" (II Peter 1:3).

Thesis #94

To be tempted does not represent a lack of faith or a deficient Christian life. **Temptation** is the enticement or solicitation of the tempter (cf. I Thess. 3:5)) to sin (James 1:14), to exhibit the character of the Evil One. God does not tempt anyone to evil (James 1:13). Temptation is not sin – Jesus was "tempted in all things as we are, yet without sin" (Heb. 4:15). "The Lord knows how to rescue the godly from temptation" (II Pet. 2:9) by the constant provision of His grace.

Thesis #95

Whereas, the human race was "created for His glory" (Isa. 43:7), the objective for humanity, both individually and collectively, must be to "do all to the glory of God" (I Cor. 10:31) – *soli gloria Deo*. God is glorified not by anything that man might attempt to do to please Him, serve Him, or exalt Him. Rather, God is glorified only when His own all-glorious character is allowed expression within His creation by the dynamic of His grace in order to bring glory to Himself.

Postscript

Our objective in drafting these ninety-five theses is not to denigrate or destroy the genuine Church of Jesus Christ, but rather to challenge the contemporary expressions of the same in such a way as to call the church back to its Christocentric reality in the risen and living Lord Jesus Christ. Please join us in the constructive discussion of the issues herein raised, and pray with us that God the Father, Son, and Holy Spirit might be glorified in all of our endeavors.

The theses enumerated above are not all essential of acceptance for personal, spiritual salvation or well-being, nor should they all be of required assent for loving fellowship and interaction among Christian brethren. Christians must **agree to disagree**, and allow for varying opinions and convictions on many issues, continuing to engage in loving discussion of the same. "In essentials unity; in non-essentials liberty, in all things love," is an historic Christian motto.

Those who have signed this document may not agree with every expression in these ninety-five theses, but they do concur that these are statements and issues that need to be addressed and discussed by Christian people at this present time in history. May this document be the starting point for an on-going discussion among Christians in Eastern Orthodox, Roman Catholic, and Protestant churches, as well as those in the many independent fellowships around the world.

Peace be with you. May God be glorified.

www.ingramcontent.com/pod-product-compliance
Lightning Source LLC
Chambersburg PA
CBHW071816020426
42331CB00007B/1500